I SPY

FALL & WINTER!

WELCOME TO

I SPY
FALL & WINTER!

GOOD LUCK!

I SPY with my little eye, something beginning with...

M is for MUSHROOM!

I SPY with my little eye, something beginning with...

S is for SNOWMAN!

I SPY with my little eye, something beginning with...

A is for APPLE!

I SPY with my little eye, something beginning with...

T is for TURKEY!

I SPY with my little eye, something beginning with...

P is for PENGUIN!

I SPY with my little eye, something beginning with...

L is for LEAF!

I SPY with my little eye, something beginning with...

H is for HOUSE!

I SPY with my little eye, something beginning with...

V is for

VAMPIRE!

I SPY with my little eye, something beginning with...

F
is for
Fox!

I SPY with my little eye, something beginning with...

i
is for
iGLoo!

I SPY with my little eye, something beginning with...

D

is for

DRUM!

I SPY with my little eye, something beginning with...

C c

is for

CANDY CANE!

I SPY with my little eye, something beginning with...

R

is for

REINDEER!

I SPY with my little eye, something beginning with...

B is for BLANKET!

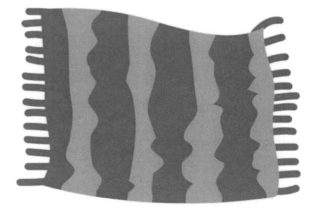

I SPY with my little eye, something beginning with...

G
is for
GINGERBREAD MAN!

I SPY with my little eye, something beginning with...

E

is for

ELF!

I SPY with my little eye, something beginning with...

W

is for

WITCH!

THE END!

Find us on Amazon!

Discover all of the titles available in the series; including these below...

I SPY ANIMALS!

I SPY LOOK and SEE!

I SPY FROM A-Z!

I SPY IN THE CITY!

I SPY AT THE SEASIDE!

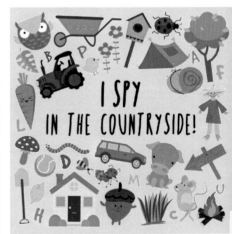

I SPY IN THE COUNTRYSIDE!

Made in United States
North Haven, CT
09 January 2022

14495154R00022